This book belongs to:

....

igloo

Published in 2010
by Igloo Books Ltd
Cottage Farm
Sywell
NN6 0BJ
www.igloo-books.com

B044 0810

10 9 8 7 6 5 4 3 2 1

ISBN 978 0 85734 4342

Designed by Insight Design Concepts Ltd

Printed and manufactured in China

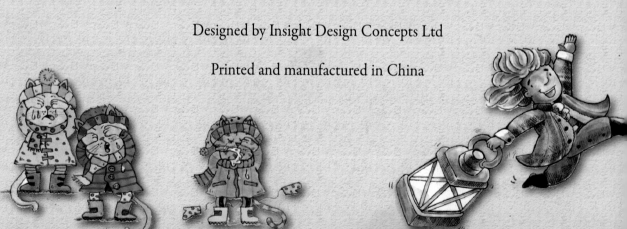

MY TREASURY OF
NURSERY RHYMES

Illustrated by Paige Billin-Frye,
Susan DeSantis,
Mernie Gallagher-Cole, Ronnie Rooney,
Carol Schwartz and Liza Woodruff

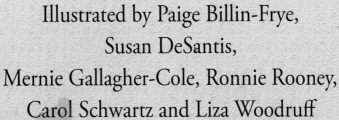

CONTENTS

Mary Had A Little Lamb

Mary had a little lamb,
Whose fleece was white as snow.
And everywhere that Mary went,
The lamb was sure to go.

He followed her to school one day,
That was against the rule.
It made the children laugh and play,
To see a lamb at school.

And so the teacher turned it out,
But still it lingered near.
And waited patiently about,
'Til Mary did appear.

"Why does the lamb love Mary so?"
The eager children cry.
"Why, Mary loves the lamb, you know,"
The teacher did reply.

Jack And Jill

Jack and Jill went up the hill,
To fetch a pail of water.
Jack fell down and broke his crown,
And Jill came tumbling after.

Up got Jack, and home did trot,
As fast as he could caper.
He went to bed and bound his head,
With vinegar and brown paper.

HEY DIDDLE DIDDLE

Hey diddle diddle,
The cat and the fiddle,
The cow jumped over the moon.

The little dog laughed,
To see such fun,
And the dish ran away,
With the spoon!

10

One For Sorrow

One for sorrow,
Two for joy,
Three for a girl,
Four for a boy,
Five for silver,
Six for gold,
Seven for a secret never to be told.
Eight for a wish,
Nine for a kiss,
Ten for a bird you should not miss.
Magpie!

Three Little Kittens

Three little kittens, they lost their mittens,
And they began to cry.
Oh, mother, dear, we sadly fear,
Our mittens we have lost.
What! Lost your mittens? You naughty kittens!
Then you shall have no pie.
Mee-ow, mee-ow, mee-ow.

Ten Little Ladybirds

One little, two little, three little ladybirds,
Four little, five little, six little ladybirds,
Seven little, eight little, nine little ladybirds,
Ten little ladybird bugs.

Ten little, nine little, eight little ladybirds,
Seven little, six little, five little ladybirds,
Four little, three little, two little ladybirds,
One little ladybird bug.

Six Little Mice

Six little mice sat down to spin.
Pussy passed by and she peeped in.
"What are you doing, my little men?"
"Weaving coats for gentlemen."
"Shall I come in and cut off your threads?"
"No, no, mistress pussy, you'd bite off our heads."
"Oh, no, I'll not; I'll help you to spin."
"That may be so,
But you don't
Come in!"

3

The Wheels On The Bus

The wheels on the bus go round and round,
Round and round, round and round.
The wheels on the bus go round and round,
All day long.

The horn on the bus goes toot toot toot,
Toot toot toot, toot toot toot.
The horn on the bus goes toot toot toot,
All day long.

The wipers on the bus go swish swish swish,
Swish swish swish, swish swish swish.
The wipers on the bus go swish swish swish,
All day long.

The people on the bus go up and down,
Up and down, up and down.
The people on the bus go up and down,
All day long.

I'm The King Of The Castle

I'm the King of the castle,
Get down you dirty rascal.
Get down, get down,
I'm the King of the castle.

London Bridge Is Falling Down

London Bridge is falling down,
Falling down, falling down.
London Bridge is falling down,
My fair lady.

15

OLD MacDONALD

Old MacDonald had a farm E-I-E-I-O.
And on that farm he had some ducks E-I-E-I-O.
With a **quack quack** here and a **quack quack** there.
Here a **quack**, there a **quack**, everywhere a **quack, quack**
Old MacDonald had a farm E-I-E-I-O.

Old MacDonald had a farm E-I-E-I-O.
And on that farm he had some cows E-I-E-I-O.
With a **moo moo** here and a **moo moo** there.
Here a **moo**, there a **moo**, everywhere a **moo, moo**.
Old MacDonald had a farm E-I-E-I-O.

Old MacDonald had a farm E-I-E-I-O.
And on that farm he had some sheep E-I-E-I-O.
With a **baa baa** here and a **baa baa** there.
Here a **baa**, there a **baa**, everywhere a **baa, baa**
Old MacDonald had a farm E-I-E-I-O.

Old MacDonald had a farm E-I-E-I-O.
And on that farm he had some pigs E-I-E-I-O.
With a **snort snort** here and a **snort snort** there.
Here a **snort**, there a **snort**, everywhere a **snort, snort**.
Old MacDonald had a farm E-I-E-I-O.

Baa, Baa, Black Sheep

Baa, baa, black sheep,
Have you any wool?
Yes, sir, yes, sir,
Three bags full.
One for my master,
And one for my dame,
And one for the little boy
Who lives down the lane.

She Sells Sea Shells

She sells sea shells on the sea shore.
The shells she sells are sea shells, I'm sure.
And if she sells sea shells on the sea shore,
Then I'm sure she sells seashore shells.

A Sailor Went To Sea

A sailor went to sea, sea, sea,
To see what he could see, see, see,
And all that he could see, see, see,
Was the bottom of the deep blue sea, sea, sea.

18

If All The Seas Were One Sea

If all the seas were one sea, what a great sea that would be.
And if all the trees were one tree, what a great tree that would be.
And if all the axes were one axe, what a great axe that would be.
And if all the men were one man, what a great man that would be.
And if the great man took the great axe, and cut down the great tree.
And let it fall into the great sea, what a splish splash that would be.

LITTLE JACK HORNER

Little Jack Horner sat in the corner,
Eating a Christmas pie.
He put in his thumb,
And pulled out a plum,
And said, "What a good boy am I!"

POLLY PUT THE KETTLE ON

Polly put the kettle on,
Polly put the kettle on,
Polly put the kettle on,
We'll all have tea.

Sukey take it off again,
Sukey take it off again,
Sukey take it off again,
They've all gone away.

Old Mother Hubbard

Old Mother Hubbard,
Went to the cupboard,
To give her poor dog a bone.
But when she got there,
The cupboard was bare,
And so the poor dog had none.

I'm A Little Teapot

I'm a little teapot short and stout,
Here is my handle, here is my spout,
When I get all steamed, up hear me shout,
Tip me over and pour me out.

21

Five Fat Sausages

Five fat sausages sizzling in a pan,
One went pop! And the others went bang!

Four fat sausages sizzling in a pan,
One went pop! And the others went bang!

Three fat sausages sizzling in a pan,
One went pop! And the others went bang!

Two fat sausages sizzling in a pan,
One went pop! And the other went bang!

One fat sausage sizzling in a pan
One went pop! And none went bang!

No fat sausages sizzling in a pan.

Little Tommy Tucker

Little Tommy Tucker,
Sings for his supper.
What shall we give him?
White bread and butter.
How shall he cut it without any knife?
How will he marry without any wife?

Jack Sprat

Jack Sprat could eat no fat,
His wife could eat no lean,
And so between them both, you see,
They licked the platter clean.

23

BATH TIME

A rubber duck and a sailboat,
I watch my bath toys sink and float.
They keep me company in the tub,
'Til mother makes me soap and scrub.
I love to take a bath each night,
And go to bed all clean and bright.

24

GOOSEY, GOOSEY, GANDER

Goosey, goosey, gander,
Wither shall I wander,
Upstairs and downstairs,
And in my lady's chamber.
There I met an old man,
Who would not say his prayers.
I took him by the left leg,
And threw him down the stairs.

25

DING DONG BELL

Ding dong bell.
Pussy's in the well.
Who put her in?
Little Tommy Thin.
Who pulled her out?
Little Tommy Stout.
What a naughty boy was that,
To drown poor pussy cat,
Who ne'er did any harm,
But killed all the mice in father's barn.

One Man Went To Mow

One man went to mow, went to mow a meadow,
One man and his dog,
Went to mow a meadow.

Two men went to mow, went to mow a meadow,
Two men, one man and his dog,
Went to mow a meadow.

Three men went to mow, went to mow a meadow,
Three men, two men, one man and his dog,
Went to mow a meadow.

Four men went to mow, went to mow a meadow,
Four men, three men, two men, one man and his dog,
Went to mow a meadow.

Little Boy Blue

Little Boy Blue, come, blow your horn!
The sheep's in the meadow, the cow's in the corn.
Where's the little boy that looks after the sheep?
Under the haystack, fast asleep.

LITTLE POLLY FLINDERS

Little Polly Flinders,
Sat among the cinders,
Warming her pretty little toes.

Her mother came and caught her,
And told her little daughter off,
For spoiling her nice new clothes.

DOODLE, DOODLE, DOO

Doodle, doodle, doo,
The princess lost her shoe.
Her highness hopped,
The fiddler stopped,
Not knowing what to do.

29

THE FARMER'S IN HIS DEN

The farmer's in his den,
The farmer's in his den,
E-I-E-I-O, the farmer's in his den.

The farmer wants a wife,
The farmer wants a wife,
E-I-E-I-O, the farmer wants a wife.

The wife wants a child,
The wife wants a child,
E-I-E-I-O, the wife wants a child.

The child wants a nurse,
The child wants a nurse,
E-I-E-I-O, the child wants a nurse.

The nurse wants a dog,
The nurse wants a dog,
E-I-E-I-O, the nurse wants a dog.

The dog wants a bone,
The dog wants a bone,
E-I-E-I-O, the dog wants a bone.

We all pat the bone,
We all pat the bone,
E-I-E-I-O, we all pat the bone.

THE COCK CROWS

The cock crows in the morn,
To tell us to rise,
And he that lies late,
Will never be wise.

For early to bed,
And early to rise,
Is the way to be healthy,
And wealthy and wise.

LITTLE BO-PEEP

Little Bo-Peep has lost her sheep,
And can't tell where to find them.
Leave them alone, and they'll come home,
And bring their tails behind them.

31

THE ANTS GO MARCHING

The ants go marching one by one,
Hurray! Hurray!
The ants go marching one by one,
Hurray! Hurray!
The ants go marching one by one,
The little one stops to suck her thumb,
And they all go marching down,
To the ground,
To get out, of the rain,
Boom, boom, boom, boom!

The ants go marching two by two,
Hurray! Hurray!
The ants go marching two by two,
Hurray! Hurray!
The ants go marching two by two,
The little one stops to tie her shoe,
And they all go marching down,
To the ground,
To get out, of the rain,
Boom, boom, boom, boom!

Rain On The Green Grass

Rain on the green grass,
And rain on the tree.
Rain on the roof-top,
But not on me.

Jenny Wren

As little Jenny Wren,
Was sitting by the shed.
She waggled with her tail,
And nodded with her head.

She waggled with her tail,
And nodded with her head.
As little Jenny Wren,
Was sitting by the shed.

An Apple A Day

An apple a day,
Sends the doctor away.

An apple in the morning,
Doctor's warning!

Roast apple at night,
Starves the doctor outright.

Eat an apple going to bed,
Knock the doctor on the head.

Three each day, seven days a week,
Ruddy apple, ruddy cheek!

DOCTOR FOSTER

Doctor Foster went to Gloucester,
In a shower of rain.
He stepped in a puddle,
Right up to his middle,
And never went there again.

DOCTOR BELL

Doctor Bell,
Fell down the well,
And broke his collar bone.
Doctors should
Attend the sick,
And leave the well alone.

Cackle, Cackle

Cackle, cackle, mother goose,
Have you any feathers loose?
Truly have I, pretty fellow,
Half enough to fill a pillow.
Here are quills, take one or two,
And down to make a bed for you.

The Clever Hen

I had a little hen, the prettiest ever seen,
She washed me the dishes and kept the house clean.
She went to the mill to fetch me some flour,
She brought it home in less than an hour.
She baked me my bread, she brewed me my ale,
She sat by the fire and told many a fine tale.

A CAT CAME FIDDLING

A cat came fiddling out of a barn,
With a pair of bagpipes under her arm.
She could sing nothing but fiddle dee dee,
The mouse has married the bumblebee.
Pipe cat, dance mouse,
We'll have a wedding at our good house.

HIGGELTY, PIGGELTY, POP!

Higgelty, piggelty, pop!
The dog has eaten the mop.
The pig's in a hurry,
The cat's in a flurry,
Higgelty, piggelty, pop!

37

SOLOMON GRUNDY

Solomon Grundy,
Born on a Monday,
Christened on Tuesday,
Married on Wednesday,
Took ill on Thursday,
Worse on Friday,
Died on Saturday,
Buried on Sunday,
This is the end,
Of Solomon Grundy.

TOMMY SNOOKS

As Tommy Snooks and Bessy Brooks,
Were walking out one Sunday.
Says Tommy Snooks to Bessy Brooks,
"Wilt marry me on Monday?"

BESSY BELL AND MARY GRAY

Bessy Bell and Mary Gray,
They were two bonny lasses.
They built their house upon the lea,
And covered it with rashes.

Bessy kept the garden gate,
And Mary kept the pantry.
Bessy always had to wait,
While Mary lived in plenty.

39

POP! GOES THE WEASEL

All around the carpenter's bench,
The monkey chased the weasel.
That's the way,
The monkey goes,
Pop! Goes the weasel.

40

CROSS PATCH

Cross Patch,
Draw the latch,
Sit by the fire and spin.
Take a cup and drink it up,
Then call your neighbors in.

The House That Jack Built

This is the house
That Jack built.

This is the malt,
That lay in the house,
That Jack built.

This is the rat,
That ate the malt,
That lay in the house,
That Jack built.

This is the cat,
That killed the rat,
That ate the malt,
That lay in the house,
That Jack built.

This is the dog,
That worried the cat,
That killed the rat,
That ate the malt,
That lay in the house,
That Jack built.

This is the cow with the crumpled horn,
That tossed the dog,
That worried the cat,
That killed the rat,
That ate the malt,
That lay in the house
That Jack built.

This is the maiden all forlorn,
That milked the cow with the crumpled horn,
That tossed the dog,
That worried the cat,
That killed the rat,
That ate the malt,
That lay in the house
That Jack built.

This is the man all tattered and torn,
That kissed the maiden all forlorn,
That milked the cow with the crumpled horn,
That tossed the dog,
That worried the cat,
That killed the rat,
That ate the malt,
That lay in the house
That Jack built.

This is the priest all shaven and shorn,
That married the man all tattered and torn,
That kissed the maiden all forlorn,
That milked the cow with the crumpled horn,
That tossed the dog,
That worried the cat,
That killed the rat,
That ate the malt,
That lay in the house
That Jack built.

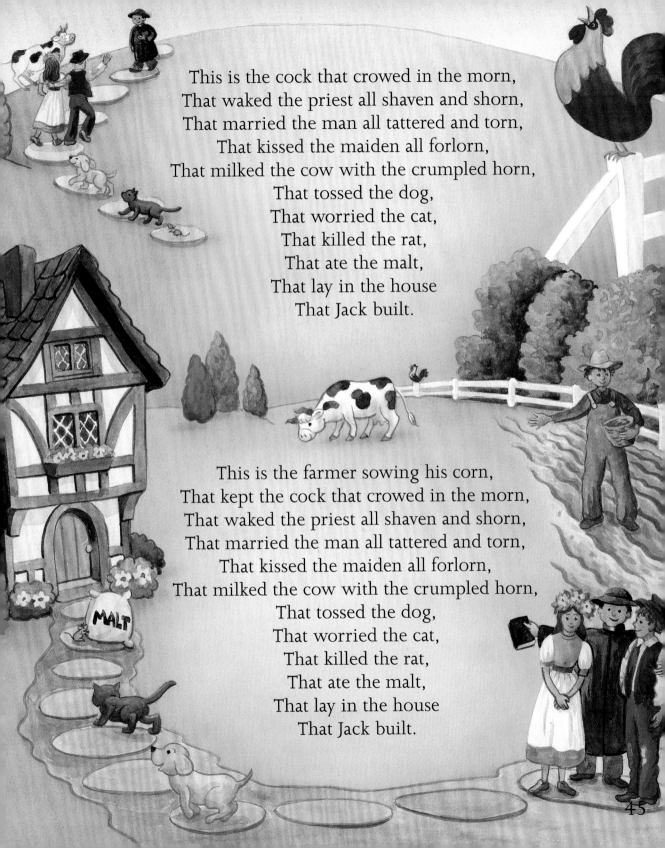

This is the cock that crowed in the morn,
That waked the priest all shaven and shorn,
That married the man all tattered and torn,
That kissed the maiden all forlorn,
That milked the cow with the crumpled horn,
That tossed the dog,
That worried the cat,
That killed the rat,
That ate the malt,
That lay in the house
That Jack built.

This is the farmer sowing his corn,
That kept the cock that crowed in the morn,
That waked the priest all shaven and shorn,
That married the man all tattered and torn,
That kissed the maiden all forlorn,
That milked the cow with the crumpled horn,
That tossed the dog,
That worried the cat,
That killed the rat,
That ate the malt,
That lay in the house
That Jack built.

45

Birds Of A Feather

Birds of a feather flock together,
And so do pigs and swine.
Rats and mice will have their choice,
And so will l have mine.

My Black Hen

Hickety pickety, my black hen,
She lays eggs for gentlemen,
Sometimes nine, sometimes ten,
Hickety pickety, my black hen.

46

Animal Fair

I went to the animal fair,
The birds and the beasts were there,
The big baboon by the light of the moon,
Was combing his auburn hair.

You ought to have seen the monkey,
He jumped on the elephant's trunk.
The elephant sneezed and fell on his knees,
And what became of the monkey? Poor monkey.

47

I Had A Little Nut Tree

I had a little nut tree,
Nothing would it bear.
But a silver nutmeg,
And a golden pear.
The King of Spain's daughter,
Came to visit me.
And all for the sake,
Of my little nut tree.

Her dress was made of crimson,
Jet black was her hair.
She asked me for my nut tree,
And my golden pear.
I said, "So fair a princess,
Never did I see.
I'll give you all the fruit,
From my little nut tree."

THE GRAND OLD DUKE OF YORK

The grand old Duke of York,
He had ten thousand men.
He marched them up to the top of the hill,
And he marched them down again.

And when they were up, they were up,
And when they were down, they were down,
And when they were only halfway up,
They were neither up nor down!

49

I Had A Little Pony,

I had a little pony his name was Dapple Gray.
I lent him to a lady to ride a mile away.
She whipped him, she thrashed him,
She rode him through the mire.
Now I would not lend my pony to any lady hire.

This Is The Way The Ladies Ride

This is the way the ladies ride,
Tri, tre, tre, tree!
Tri, tre, tre, tree!
This is the way the ladies ride,
Tri, tre, tre, tre, tri-tre-tre-tree!

This is the way the gentlemen ride,
Gallop-a-trot!
Gallop-a-trot!
This is the way the gentlemen ride,
Gallop-a-gallop-a-trot!

50

A Farmer Went Trotting

A farmer went trotting upon his bay mare,
Bumpety, bumpety, bump!
With his daughter behind, so rosy and fair,
Bumpety, bumpety, bump!
A raven cried, "Croak!" and they went tumbling down,
Bumpety, bumpety, bump!
The mare broke her knees and the farmer his crown,
Bumpety, bumpety, bump!
The mischievous raven flew laughing away,
Bumpety, bumpety, bump!
And vowed he would serve them the same the next day,
Lumpety, lumpety, lump!

Star Light, Star Bright

Star light, star bright,
The first star I see tonight,
I wish I may, I wish I might,
Have the wish I wish tonight.

Sleep, Baby, Sleep

Sleep, baby, sleep,
Your father tends the sheep,
Your mother shakes the dreamland tree,
And from it fall sweet dreams for thee.
Sleep, baby, sleep.
Sleep, baby, sleep.

The Man In The Moon

The man in the moon came tumbling down,
And asked the way to Norwich.
He went by the south, and burnt his mouth,
With eating cold pease porridge.

Early To Bed

Early to bed,
Early to rise.
Makes little Johnny,
Wealthy and wise.

SIMPLE SIMON

Simple Simon met a pieman,
Going to the fair.
Says Simple Simon to the pieman,
"Let me taste your ware."

Says the pieman to Simple Simon,
"Show me first your penny,"
Says Simple Simon to the pieman,
"Indeed, I have not any."

Simple Simon went a-fishing,
For to catch a whale.
All the water he could find,
Was in his mother's pail!

Simple Simon went to look,
If plums grew on a thistle.
He pricked his fingers very much,
Which made poor Simon whistle.

He went to catch a dicky bird,
And thought he could not fail.
Because he had a little salt,
To put upon its tail.

He went for water with a sieve,
But soon it ran all through.
And now poor Simple Simon,
Bids you all adieu.

54

Up The Wooden Hill

Up the wooden hill to Blanket Fair,
What shall we have when we get there?
A bucket full of water,
And a penny-worth of hay,
Gee up, Dobbin, all the way!

Girls Are Dandy

Girls are dandy, made of candy,
That's what little girls are made of.
Boys are rotten, made of cotton,
That's what little boys are made of.

55

Incy Wincy Spider

Incy wincy spider climbed up the water spout,
Down came the rain and washed the spider out,
Out came the sun and dried up all the rain,
So incy wincy spider climbed up the spout again.

THE CROOKED SIXPENCE

There was a crooked man, and he went a crooked mile,
He found a crooked sixpence beside a crooked stile,
He bought a crooked cat, which caught a crooked mouse,
And they all lived together in a little crooked house.

MY HEAD

This is the circle,
That is my head.
This is my mouth,
With which words are said.
These are my eyes,
With which I see.
This is my nose,
That's a part of me.
This is the hair,
That grows on my head.
And this is my hat,
All pretty and red.

58

Bat, Bat, Come Under My Hat

Bat, bat, come under my hat,
And I'll give you a slice of bacon.
And when I bake,
I'll give you a cake,
If I am not mistaken.

Three Young Rats

Three young rats with black felt hats,
Three young ducks with white straw flats,
Three young dogs with curling tails,
Three young cats with demi-veils,
Went out to walk with two young pigs,
In satin vests and sorrel wigs,
But suddenly it chanced to rain,
And so they all went home again.

59

Rain, Rain, Go Away

Rain, rain, go away,
Come again another day,
Little Johnny wants to play.

Georgie Porgie

Georgie Porgie pudding and pie,
Kissed the girls and made them cry.
When the boys came out to play,
Georgie Porgie ran away.

Kookaburra

Kookaburra sits on an old gum tree,
Merry, merry king of the bush is he.
Laugh, kookaburra, laugh, kookaburra,
Gay your life must be.

A Tisket, A Tasket

A tisket, a tasket,
A green and yellow basket.
I wrote a letter to my love,
But on the way I dropped it.
I dropped it, I dropped it,
And, on the way I dropped it.
A little boy picked it up,
And put it in his pocket.

61

THE OWL AND THE PUSSYCAT

The owl and the pussycat went to sea,
In a beautiful pea-green boat.
They took some honey, and plenty of money,
Wrapped up in a five-pound note.

The owl looked up to the stars above,
And sang to a small guitar.
"O lovely pussy, O pussy my love,
What a beautiful pussy you are, you are!
What a beautiful pussy you are!"

Pussy said to the owl "You elegant fowl,
How charmingly sweet you sing!
Oh! let us be married, too long we have tarried,
But what shall we do for a ring?"

They sailed away, for a year and a day,
To the land where the bong-tree grows.
And there in a wood a piggy-wig stood,
With a ring at the end of his nose, his nose,
With a ring at the end of his nose.

"Dear pig, are you willing to sell for one shilling,
Your ring?" said the piggy "I will."
So they took it away and were married next day,
By the turkey who lives on the hill.

They dined on mince and slices of quince,
Which they ate with a runcible spoon.
And hand in hand on the edge of the sand,
They danced by the light of the moon, the moon
They danced by the light of the moon.

LITTLE NANCY ETTICOAT

Little Nancy Etticoat,
With a white petticoat,
And a red nose.
She has no feet or hands,
The longer she stands,
The shorter she grows.

IT'S RAINING, IT'S POURING

It's raining, it's pouring,
The old man is snoring.
He went to bed,
And bumped his head,
And couldn't get up in the morning.

SOMEONE CAME KNOCKING

Someone came knocking at my wee small door,
Someone came knocking, I'm sure-sure-sure.
I listened, I opened, I looked to left and right,
But nought there was a-stirring in the still dark night.

Only the busy beetle tap-tapping in the wall,
Only from the forest the screech-owl's call,
Only the cricket whistling while the dew drops fall,
So I know not who came knocking, at all, at all, at all.

65

FIVE LITTLE DUCKS

Five little ducks
Went out one day,
Over the hill and far away.
Mother duck said,
"Quack, quack, quack, quack."
But only four little ducks came back.

Four little ducks
Went out one day,
Over the hill and far away.
Mother duck said,
"Quack, quack, quack, quack."
But only three little ducks came back.

Three little ducks
Went out one day,
Over the hill and far away.
Mother duck said,
"Quack, quack, quack, quack."
But only two little ducks came back.

Two little ducks
Went out one day,
Over the hill and far away.
Mother duck said,
"Quack, quack, quack, quack."
But only one little duck came back.

Row, Row, Row Your Boat

Row, row, row your boat,
Gently down the stream.
Merrily, merrily, merrily,
Life is but a dream.

Row, row, row your boat,
Gently down the stream.
If you see a crocodile,
Don't forget to scream.

One little duck
Went out one day,
Over the hill and far away.
Mother duck said,
"Quack, quack, quack, quack."
And all of the five little ducks came back.

67

To Market

To market, to market, to buy a fat pig,
Home again, home again, jiggety jig.

To market, to market, to buy a fat hog,
Home again, home again, jiggety jog.

To market, to market, to buy a plum bun,
Home again, home again, market is done.

THE MUFFIN MAN

Oh do you know the Muffin Man,
The Muffin Man,
The Muffin Man?
Do you know the Muffin Man
That lives in Drury Lane?

Oh yes I know the Muffin Man,
The Muffin Man,
The Muffin Man.
Yes l know the Muffin Man
That lives in Drury Lane.

HOT-CROSS BUNS

Hot-cross buns, hot-cross buns!
One a-penny, two a-penny,
Hot-cross buns!

Dance to Your Daddy

Dance to your daddy,
My bonnie laddy,
Dance to your daddy,
My bonnie lamb.

You shall get a fishy,
In a little dishy,
You shall have a fishy,
When the boat comes in.

You shall get a coatie,
And a pair of breeches,
And you'll get an eggy,
And a bit of ham.

THE BIG SHIP SAILS

The big ship sails,
On the alley, alley oh.
The alley, alley oh.
The big ship sails,
On the alley, alley oh.
On the last day of December.

WASH ON MONDAY

Wash on Monday,
Iron on Tuesday,
Bake on Wednesday,
Brew on Thursday,
Churn on Friday,
Mend on Saturday,
Meeting on Sunday.

PEASE PORRIDGE

Pease porridge hot,
Pease porridge cold,
Pease porridge in the pot,
Nine days old.
Some like it hot,
Some like it cold,
Some like it in the pot,
Nine days old.

PAT-A-CAKE

Pat-a-cake, pat-a-cake,
Baker's man.
Bake me a cake,
As fast as you can.
Roll it, and poke it,
And mark it with B.
And throw it in the oven,
For baby and me.

I'm a Dingly Dangly Scarecrow

I'm a dingly dangly scarecrow,
With a flippy floppy hat.
I can shake my hands like this,
I can shake my feet like that.

THE NORTH WIND DOTH BLOW

The north wind doth blow,
And we shall have snow,
And what will poor robin do then,
Poor thing?
He'll sit in a barn,
And keep himself warm,
And hide his head under his wing,
Poor thing!

My Shadow

I have a little shadow,
That goes in and out with me.
And what can be the use of him,
Is more than I can see.
He is very, very like me,
From the heels up to the head.
And I see him jump before me,
When I jump into my bed.

The funniest thing about him,
Is the way he likes to grow.
Not at all like proper children,
Which is always very slow.
For he sometimes shoots up taller,
Like an india-rubber ball.
And he sometimes goes so little,
That there's none of him at all.

Ring-A-Ring O'Roses

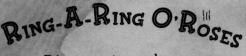

Ring-a-ring o'roses,
A pocket full of posies,
Atishoo! Atishoo!
We all fall down.

SEE-SAW, MARGERY DAW

See-saw, Margery Daw,
Jacky shall have a new master.
He shall have but a penny a day,
Because he can't work any faster.

THIS LITTLE PIGGY

This little piggy went to market,
This little piggy stayed at home,
This little piggy had roast beef,
This little piggy had none.
And this little piggy went...
"Wee wee wee," all the way home.

TOM, TOM, THE PIPER'S SON

Tom, Tom, the piper's son,
Stole a pig and away he ran.
The pig was eat,
And Tom was beat,
And Tom went howling down the street.

78

BARBER, BARBER

Barber, barber, shave a pig!
How many hairs to make a wig?
Four and twenty, that's enough!
Give the barber a pinch of snuff.

GREGORY GRIGGS

Gregory Griggs,
Gregory Griggs,
Had forty-seven,
Different wigs.

He wore them up,
He wore them down,
To please the people,
Of Boston town.

He wore them east,
He wore them west,
But he could never tell,
Which he loved best.

AIKEN DRUM

There was a man lived in the moon,
Lived in the moon, lived in the moon.
There was a man lived in the moon,
And his name was Aiken Drum.

And he played upon a ladle, a ladle, a ladle,
And he played upon a ladle,
And his name was Aiken Drum.

And his hat was made of good cream cheese,
Of good cream cheese, of good cream cheese.
And his hat was made of good cream cheese,
And his name was Aiken Drum.

And he played upon a ladle, a ladle, a ladle,
And he played upon a ladle.
And his name was Aiken Drum.

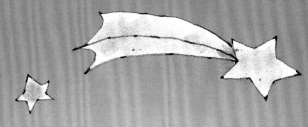

And his coat was made of good roast beef,
Of good roast beef, of good roast beef.
And his coat was made of good roast beef,
And his name was Aiken Drum.

And he played upon a ladle, a ladle, a ladle,
And he played upon a ladle.
And his name was Aiken Drum.

And his buttons made of penny loaves,
Of penny loaves, of penny loaves.
And his buttons made of penny loaves,
And his name was Aiken Drum.

And he played upon a ladle, a ladle, a ladle,
And he played upon a ladle.
And his name was Aiken Drum.

And his breeches made of haggis bags,
Of haggis bags, of haggis bags.
And his breeches made of haggis bags,
And his name was Aiken Drum.

Up In The Green Orchard

Up in the green orchard,
There is a green tree.
The finest of pippins,
That you may see.
The apples are ripe,
And ready to fall,
And Robin and Richard,
Shall gather them all.

Blow Wind, Blow

Blow wind, blow! And go mill, go!
That the miller may grind his corn.
That the baker may take it,
And into bread make it,
And bring us a loaf in the morn.

A Duck And A Drake

A duck and a drake,
And a nice barley cake,
With a penny to pay the old baker.
A hop and a scotch,
Is another notch,
Slitherum, slatherum, take her.

WHERE ARE YOU GOING, MY PRETTY MAID?

"Where are you going, my pretty maid?"
"I'm going a-milking, sir," she said.
"May I go with you, my pretty maid?"
"You're kindly welcome, sir," she said.
"What is your father, my pretty maid?"
"My father's a farmer, sir," she said.

"Say, will you marry me, my pretty maid?"
"Yes, if you please, kind sir," she said.
"What is your fortune, my pretty maid?"
"My face is my fortune, sir," she said.
"Then I can't marry you, my pretty maid!"
"Nobody asked you, sir," she said.

GOING TO ST. IVES

As I was going to St. Ives I met a man with seven wives.
Each wife had seven sacks, each sack had seven cats,
Each cat had seven kittens: kittens, cats, sacks and wives.
How many were going to St. Ives?

PRETTY MAID

Pretty maid, pretty maid,
Where have you been?
Gathering a posie,
To give to the Queen.

Pretty maid, pretty maid,
What gave she you?
She gave me a diamond,
As big as my shoe.

OLD KING COLE

Old King Cole,
Was a merry old soul,
And a merry old soul was he.

He called for his pipe,
And he called for his bowl,
And he called for his fiddlers three!

And every fiddler, he had a fine fiddle,
And a very fine fiddle had he.
"Twee tweedle dee, tweedle dee,"
Went the fiddlers three.

Oh, there's none so rare,
As can compare,
With King Cole and his fiddlers three.

The Queen of Hearts,
She made some tarts,
All on a summer's day.

The Knave of Hearts,
He stole those tarts,
And took them clean away.

The King of Hearts,
Called for the tarts,
And beat the Knave full sore.

The Knave of Hearts,
Brought back the tarts,
And vowed he'd steal no more.

RED SKY AT NIGHT

Red sky at night,
Shepherd's delight.
Red sky in the morning,
Shepherd's warning.

The Bear Went Over The Mountain

The bear went over the mountain,
Thc bear went over the mountain,
The bear went over the mountain,
  To see what he could see.

And all that he could see,
And all that he could see,
Was the other side of the mountain,
The other side of the mountain,
The other side of the mountain,
  Was all that he could see.

89

BUTTERFLY, BUTTERFLY

Butterfly, butterfly, flutter around.
Butterfly, butterfly, touch the ground.
Butterfly, butterfly, fly so free.
Butterfly, butterfly, land on me!
Butterfly, butterfly, reach the sky,
Butterfly, butterfly, say good-bye!

LUCY LOCKET

Lucy Locket lost her pocket,
Kitty Fisher found it.
Not a penny was there in it,
Only ribbon round it.

90

THE LITTLE GIRL

There was a little girl who had a little curl,
Right in the middle of her forehead.
When she was good, she was very, very good,
But when she was bad, she was horrid.

Draw A Pail Of Water

Draw a pail of water,
For my lady's daughter.
Her father's a king and her mother's a queen,
Her two little sisters are dressed in green,
Stamping grass and parsley,
Marigold-leaves and daises,
One rush, two rush!
Pray thee, fine lady, come under my bush.

Pussycat, Pussycat

Pussycat, pussycat, where have you been?
I've been to London to visit the Queen.
Pussycat, pussycat, what did you do there?
I frightened a little mouse under her chair.

The King Of France

The King of France went up the hill,
With twenty thousand men.
The King of France came down the hill,
And ne'er went up again.

HUSH-A-BYE

Hush-a-bye, baby, on the tree top,
When the wind blows the cradle will rock,
When the bough breaks the cradle will fall,
Down will come baby, bough, cradle and all.

THE APPLE TREE

Here is the tree with leaves so green,
Here are the apples that hang between.
When the wind blows, the apples fall,
Here is a basket to gather them all.

A Swarm Of Bees

A swarm of bees in May,
Is worth a load of hay.
A swarm of bees in June,
Is worth a silver spoon.
A swarm of bees in July,
Is not worth a fly.

Miss Muffet

Little Miss Muffet,
Sat on a tuffet,
Eating her curds and whey.
There came a big spider,
And sat down beside her,
And frightened Miss Muffet away.

95

THIS IS THE SUN

This is the sun,
So big and round.
This is a seed,
So snug in the ground.
These are the flowers,
That wave in the breeze.
These are the yachts,
That sail on the seas.

THERE WAS A LITTLE TURTLE

There was a little turtle,
Who lived in a box.
He swam in puddles,
And climbed on rocks.
He snapped at the mosquito,
He snapped at the flea,
He snapped at the minnow,
And he snapped at me.
He caught the mosquito,
He caught the flea,
He caught the minnow,
But he didn't catch me!

THREE WISE MEN

Three wise men of Gotham,
Went to sea in a bowl.
If the bowl had been stronger,
My song would have been longer.

97

Here We Go Gathering Nuts In May

Here we go gathering nuts in May,
Nuts in May, nuts in May.
Here we go gathering nuts in May,
On a cold and frosty morning.

Who will you have for nuts in May,
Nuts in May, nuts in May?
Who will you have for nuts in May,
On a cold and frosty morning.

Who will you send to fetch her away,
Fetch her away, fetch her away?
Who will you send to fetch her away,
On a cold and frosty morning?

Wills and Jack will fetch her away,
Fetch her away, fetch her away,
Wills and Jack will fetch her away,
On a cold and frosty morning.

ONE MISTY MORNING

One misty, moisty morning,
When cloudy was the weather.
There I met an old man,
Clothed all in leather.
With cap under his chin,
How do you do, and how do you do,
And how do you do again?

Five Little Monkeys

Five little monkeys jumping on the bed,
One fell off and bumped his head.
Mummy called the doctor and the doctor said,
"No more monkeys jumping on the bed!"

Four little monkeys jumping on the bed,
One fell off and bumped his head.
Mummy called the doctor and the doctor said,
"No more monkeys jumping on the bed!"

Three little monkeys jumping on the bed,
One fell off and bumped his head.
Mummy called the doctor and the doctor said,
"No more monkeys jumping on the bed!"

Two little monkeys jumping on the bed,
One fell off and bumped his head.
Mummy called the doctor and the doctor said,
"No more monkeys jumping on the bed!"

One little monkey jumping on the bed,
He fell off and bumped his head.
Mummy called the doctor and the doctor said,
"No more monkeys jumping on the bed!"

No little monkeys jumping on the bed,
None fell off and bumped their head.
Mummy called the doctor and the doctor said,
"That's what you get for jumping on the bed!"

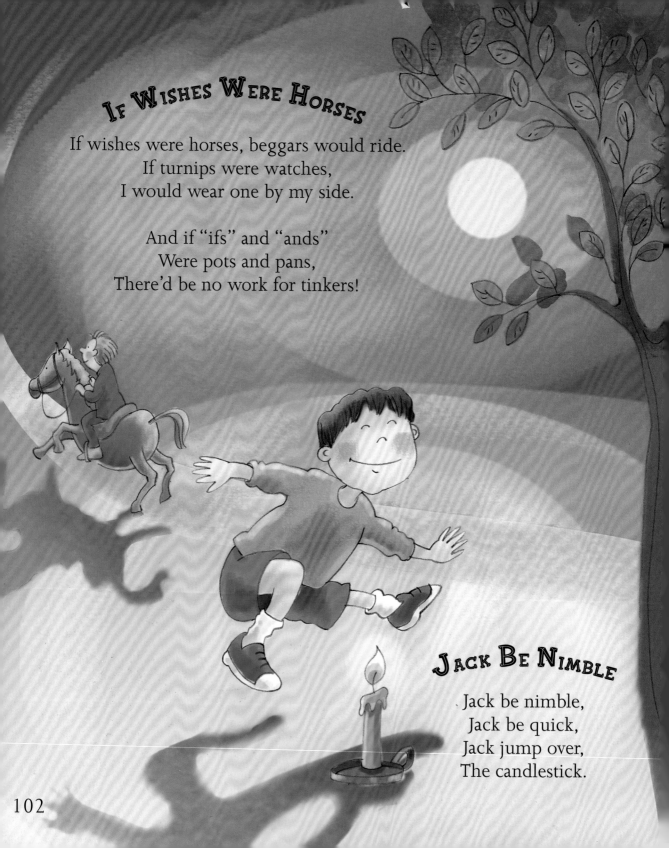

If Wishes Were Horses

If wishes were horses, beggars would ride.
If turnips were watches,
I would wear one by my side.

And if "ifs" and "ands"
Were pots and pans,
There'd be no work for tinkers!

Jack Be Nimble

Jack be nimble,
Jack be quick,
Jack jump over,
The candlestick.

How Many Miles To Babylon?

How many miles to Babylon?
Three score and ten.
Can I get there by candlelight?
Aye, and back again.
If your feet are nimble and light,
You'll get there by candlelight.

The Mulberry Bush

Here we go round the mulberry bush,
The mulberry bush, the mulberry bush.
Here we go round the mulberry bush,
So early in the morning.

Mary, Mary

Mary, Mary quite contrary,
How does your garden grow?
With silver bells and cockle shells,
And pretty maids all in a row.

ROUND AND ROUND THE GARDEN

Round and round the garden,
Like a teddy bear.
One step, two step,
Tickle you under there.

TWO LITTLE DICKY BIRDS

Two little dicky birds,
Sat upon a wall.
One named Peter,
The other named Paul.
Fly away Peter,
Fly away Paul.
Come back Peter,
Come back Paul.

Sing A Song Of Sixpence

Sing a song of sixpence,
A pocket full of rye.
Four-and-twenty blackbirds,
Baked in a pie!

When the pie was opened,
The birds began to sing.
Was not that a dainty dish,
To set before the king?

The King was in his counting-house,
Counting out his money.
The Queen was in the parlor,
Eating bread and honey.

The maid was in the garden,
Hanging out the clothes.
When down came a blackbird,
And snapped off her nose.

Humpty Dumpty

Humpty Dumpty sat on a wall.
Humpty Dumpty had a great fall.
All the King's horses and all the King's men,
Couldn't put Humpty together again.

The Lion And The Unicorn

The lion and the unicorn,
Were fighting for the crown.
The lion beat the unicorn,
All about the town.

Some gave them white bread,
And some gave them brown.
Some gave them plum cake,
And sent them out of town.

TWEEDLEDUM AND TWEEDLEDEE

Tweedledum and Tweedledee,
Agreed to have a battle.
For Tweedledum said Tweedledee,
Had spoilt his nice new rattle.

Just then flew by a monstrous crow,
As big as a tar-barrel.
Which frightened both the heroes so,
Which quite forgot their quarrel.

LADYBIRD

Ladybird, ladybird,
Fly away home.
Your house is on fire,
And your children are all alone.

Thirty Days Hath September

Thirty days hath September,
April, June and November.
All the rest have thirty-one,
Excepting February alone,
For that has twenty-eight days clear,
And twenty-nine in each leap year.

Falling Leaves

All the leaves are falling down,
Orange, yellow, red and brown.
Falling softly as they do,
Over me and over you.
All the leaves are falling down,
Orange, yellow, red and brown.

January Brings The Snow

January brings the snow,
Makes our feet and fingers glow.

February brings the rain,
Thaws the frozen lake again.

March brings breezes sharp and shrill,
Shakes the dancing daffodil.

April brings the primrose sweet,
Scatters daisies at our feet.

May brings flocks of pretty lambs,
Skipping by their fleecy dams.

June brings tulips, lillies, roses,
Fills the children's hands with posies.

Hot July brings cooling showers,
Apricots and gilly flowers.

August brings the sheaves of corn,
Then the harvest home is borne.

Warm September brings the fruit,
Sportsmen then begin to shoot.

Brown October brings the pheasant,
Then to gather nuts is pleasant.

Dull November brings the blast,
Then the leaves go whirling past.

Chill December brings the sleet,
Blazing fire and Christmas treat.

I See The Moon

I see the moon,
And the moon sees me.
God bless the moon,
And God bless me.

Wee Willie Winkie

Wee Willie Winkie runs through the town,
Upstairs and downstairs, in his nightgown.
Rapping at the window, crying through the lock,
"Are the children in their beds,
Now it's eight o'clock?"

Boys And Girls Come Out To Play

Girls and boys, come out to play,
The moon doth shine as bright as day.
Leave your supper, and leave your sleep,
And come with your play fellows into the street.
Come with a whoop, come with a call,
Come with a good will or not at all.
Up the ladder and down the wall,
A halfpenny roll will serve us all.
You find milk, and I'll find flour,
And we'll have a pudding,
In half an hour.

Oranges And Lemons

"Oranges and lemons," say the bells of St. Clement's.
"You owe me five farthings," say the bells of St. Martin's.
"When will you pay me?" say the bells of Old Bailey.
"When I grow rich," say the bells of Shoreditch.
"When will that be?" say the bells of Stepney.
"I do not know," says the great bell at Bow.
"Here comes a candle to light you to bed.
Here comes a chopper to chop off your head.
Chip chop chip chop - the last man's dead."

Yankee Doodle

Yankee Doodle went to town,
A-riding on a pony.
He stuck a feather in his hat,
And called it macaroni.

Yankee Doodle, keep it up,
Yankee Doodle dandy.
Mind the music and the step,
And with the girls be handy.

TINKER, TAILOR

Tinker, tailor,
Soldier, sailor,
Rich man, poor man,
Beggar man,
Thief.

ONE POTATO, TWO POTATO

One potato, two potato,
Three potato, four.
Five potato, six potato,
Seven potato,
More.

117

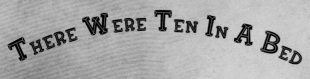

There Were Ten In A Bed

There were ten in the bed and the little one said,
"Roll over! Roll over!"
So they all rolled over and one fell out.

There were nine in the bed and the little one said,
"Roll over! Roll over!"
So they all rolled over and one fell out.

There were eight in the bed and the little one said,
"Roll over! Roll over!"
So they all rolled over and one fell out.

There were seven in the bed and the little one said,
"Roll over! Roll over!"
So they all rolled over and one fell out.

There were six in the bed and the little one said,
"Roll over! Roll over!"
So they all rolled over and one fell out.

There were five in the bed and the little one said,
"Roll over! Roll over!"
So they all rolled over and one fell out.

There were four in the bed and the little one said,
"Roll over! Roll over!"
So they all rolled over and one fell out.

There were three in the bed and the little one said,
"Roll over! Roll over!"
So they all rolled over and one fell out.

There were two in the bed and the little one said,
"Roll over! Roll over!"
So they all rolled over and one fell out.

There was one in the bed and the little one said,
"Good night!"

CHRISTMAS TREE

I'm a little Christmas tree,
Green and bright,
Here is my tinsel, here are my lights,
When I'm all fancy I think I might,
Wait for Santa to come tonight.

GINGERBREAD

Mix and stir and pat it in the pan,
I'm going to make a gingerbread man.
With a nose so neat,
And a smile so sweet,
And gingerbread shoes,
On his gingerbread feet.

Christmas Is Coming

Christmas is coming, the geese are getting fat,
Please to put a penny in an old man's hat.
If you haven't got a penny a ha'penny will do,
If you haven't got a ha'penny, God bless you.

Christmas

Christmas comes,
But once a year.
And when it comes,
It brings good cheer.

123

COME TO THE WINDOW

Come to the window,
My baby, with me,
And look at the stars,
That shine on the sea!

There are two little stars,
That play bo-peep.
With two little fishes,
Far down in the deep.

And two little frogs,
Cry "Neap, neap, neap."
I see a dear baby,
That should be asleep.

DIDDLE DIDDLE DUMPLING

Diddle diddle dumpling, my son John,
Went to bed with his breeches on.
One stocking off, and one stocking on,
Diddle diddle dumpling, my son John.

THE MOON

The moon is round,
As round can be.
Two eyes, a nose and a mouth,
Like me!

TWINKLE, TWINKLE, LITTLE STAR

Twinkle, twinkle, little star,
How I wonder what you are.
Up above the world so high,
Like a diamond in the sky.
Twinkle, twinkle, little star,
How I wonder what you are.

Teddy Bears Picnic

If you go down to the woods today,
You're in for a big surprise.
If you go down to the woods today,
You'll never believe your eyes.
For every bear that ever there was,
Is gathered there for certain because,
Today's the day the teddy bears have their picnic.

FUZZY WUZZY

Fuzzy Wuzzy was a bear.
Fuzzy Wuzzy had no hair.
So, Fuzzy Wuzzy wasn't really fuzzy,
Was he?

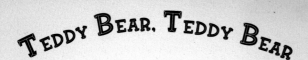

TEDDY BEAR, TEDDY BEAR

Teddy bear, teddy bear, turn around,
Teddy bear, teddy bear, touch the ground.
Teddy bear, teddy bear, show your shoe,
Teddy bear, teddy bear, that will do!

Teddy bear, teddy bear, go upstairs,
Teddy bear, teddy bear, say your prayers.
Teddy bear, teddy bear, turn out the lights,
Teddy bear, teddy bear, say good-night!

125

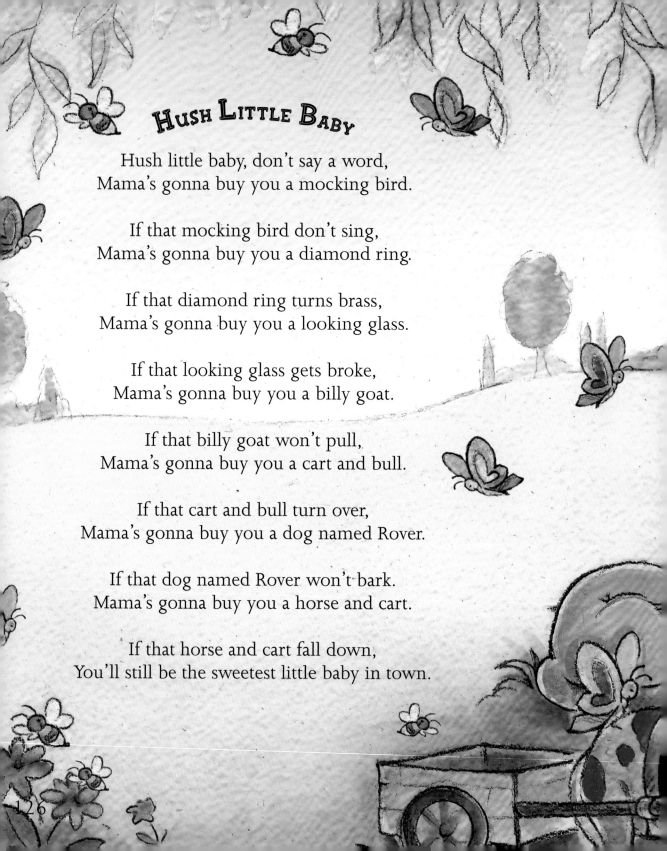

HUSH LITTLE BABY

Hush little baby, don't say a word,
Mama's gonna buy you a mocking bird.

If that mocking bird don't sing,
Mama's gonna buy you a diamond ring.

If that diamond ring turns brass,
Mama's gonna buy you a looking glass.

If that looking glass gets broke,
Mama's gonna buy you a billy goat.

If that billy goat won't pull,
Mama's gonna buy you a cart and bull.

If that cart and bull turn over,
Mama's gonna buy you a dog named Rover.

If that dog named Rover won't bark.
Mama's gonna buy you a horse and cart.

If that horse and cart fall down,
You'll still be the sweetest little baby in town.

BYE, BABY BUNTING

Bye, baby bunting,
Daddy's gone a-hunting,
To get a little rabbit skin,
To wrap my baby bunting in.

BANBURY CROSS

Ride a cock-horse,
To Banbury Cross,
To see an old lady,
Upon a white horse.

Rings on her fingers,
And bells on her toes.
She shall have music,
Wherever she goes.

LITTLE BETTY BLUE

Little Betty Blue lost her holiday shoe.
What can little Betty do?
Give her another to match the other,
And then she may walk in two.

PINS

See a pin and pick it up,
All the day you'll have good luck.
See a pin and let it lay,
Bad luck you'll have all the day.

129

LITTLE BOYS

What are little boys made of?
What are little boys made of?
Slugs and snails
And puppy dog tails,
That's what little boys are made of.

MONDAY'S CHILD

Monday's child is fair of face,
Tuesday's child is full of grace,
Wednesday's child is full of woe,
Thursday's child has far to go,
Friday's child is loving and giving,
Saturday's child must work hard for a living,
But the child who is born on the Sabbath day,
Is bonny and blithe and good and gay.

LITTLE GIRLS

What are little girls made of?
What are little girls made of?
Sugar and spice,
And all things nice.
That's what little girls are made of.

ALL WORK AND NO PLAY

All work and no play,
Makes Jack a dull boy.
All play and no work,
Makes Jack a mere toy.

HERE WE GO LOOBY LOO

Here we go looby loo,
Here we go looby light,
Here we go looby loo,
All on a Saturday night.

DAFFY DOWN DILLY

Daffy down dilly,
Has come to town.
In a yellow petticoat,
And a green gown.

THE BUNCH OF BLUE RIBBONS

Oh, dear, what can the matter be?
Oh, dear, what can the matter be?
Oh, dear, what can the matter be?
Johnny's so long at the fair.

He promised he'd buy me a bunch of blue ribbons,
He promised he'd buy me a bunch of blue ribbons,
He promised he'd buy me a bunch of blue ribbons,
To tie up my bonny brown hair.

133

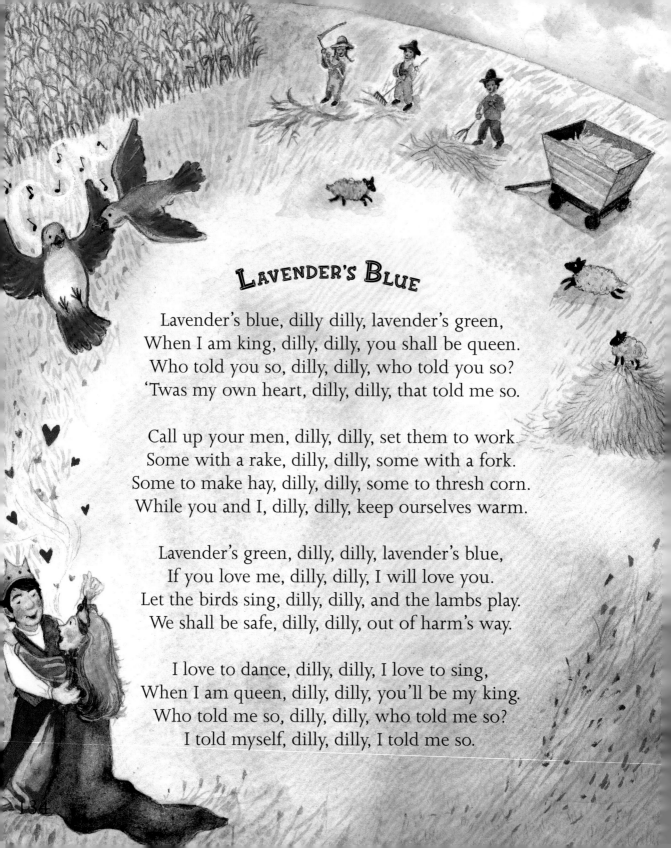

LAVENDER'S BLUE

Lavender's blue, dilly dilly, lavender's green,
When I am king, dilly, dilly, you shall be queen.
Who told you so, dilly, dilly, who told you so?
'Twas my own heart, dilly, dilly, that told me so.

Call up your men, dilly, dilly, set them to work
Some with a rake, dilly, dilly, some with a fork.
Some to make hay, dilly, dilly, some to thresh corn.
While you and I, dilly, dilly, keep ourselves warm.

Lavender's green, dilly, dilly, lavender's blue,
If you love me, dilly, dilly, I will love you.
Let the birds sing, dilly, dilly, and the lambs play.
We shall be safe, dilly, dilly, out of harm's way.

I love to dance, dilly, dilly, I love to sing,
When I am queen, dilly, dilly, you'll be my king.
Who told me so, dilly, dilly, who told me so?
I told myself, dilly, dilly, I told me so.

LITTLE COCK SPARROW

A little cock sparrow sat on a green tree,
And he chirruped, he chirruped, so merry was he.
A naughty boy came with his wee bow and arrow,
Determined to shoot this little cock sparrow.

"This little cock sparrow shall make me a stew,
And his giblets shall make me a little pie too."
"Oh, no," said the sparrow, "I won't make a stew!"
So he flapped his wings, and away he flew.

135

Bow-Wow

"Bow-wow," says the dog,
"Mew, mew," says the cat,
"Grunt, grunt," goes the hog,
And "squeak" goes the rat.

"Chirp, chirp," says the sparrow,
"Caw, caw," says the crow,
"Quack, quack," says the duck,
What cuckoos say you know.

138

So, with sparrows and cuckoos,
With rats and with dogs,
With ducks and with crows,
With cats and with hogs.

A fine song I have made,
To please you my dear,
And if it's well sung,
'Twill be charming to hear.

137

I Saw Three Ships

I saw three ships come sailing by,
Come sailing by, come sailing by,
I saw three ships come sailing by,
On New Year's Day in the morning.

And what do you think was in them then,
Was in them then, was in them then?
And what do you think was in them then,
On New Year's Day in the morning.

Three pretty girls were in them then,
Were in them then, were in them then,
Three pretty girls were in them then,
On New Year's Day in the morning.

One could whistle, and one could sing,
And one could play the violin,
Such joy there was at my wedding,
On New Year's Day in the morning.

BOBBY SHAFTOE

Bobby Shaftoe went to sea,
Silver buckles on his knee.
He'll come back and marry me,
Pretty Bobby Shaftoe.

Bobby Shaftoe's fine and fair,
Combing down his auburn hair.
He's my friend for ever more,
Pretty Bobby Shaftoe.

RUB-A-DUB

Rub-a-dub-dub,
Three men in a tub,
And who do you think they be?
The butcher, the baker,
The candlestick maker.
They all sailed out to sea.

139

IF ALL THE WORLD

If all the world were apple pie,
And all the sea were ink.
And all the trees were bread and cheese,
What would we have to drink?

140

PETER, PETER, PUMPKIN EATER

Peter, Peter, pumpkin eater,
Had a wife and couldn't keep her.
He put her in a pumpkin shell,
And there he kept her very well.

141

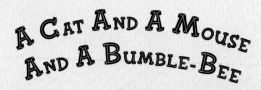

A Cat And A Mouse And A Bumble-Bee

A cat and a mouse and a bumble-bee,
Started a-dancing, one, two, three.
They danced in the daytime,
They danced in the night,
They cared not whether it was dark or light.

What did they dance to? Don't ask me!
They danced to the hum of the bumble-bee.
They danced to the purr of the big tom cat,
They danced to the mouse-squeaks high as a bat.

Where did they go to? I don't know!
Nobody ever saw them go.
But if you ask me, I'm willing to bet,
That if they are alive still, they are dancing yet.

Vintery, Mintery

Vintery, mintery, cutery, corn,
Apple seed and apple thorn,
Wire, briar, limber lock,
Three geese in a flock.

One flew east,
And one flew west,
And one flew over,
The cuckoo's nest.

Tommy Tittlemouse

Little Tommy Tittlemouse,
Lived in a little house.
He caught fishes,
In other men's ditches.

143

ONE, TWO, BUCKLE MY SHOE

One, two,
Buckle my shoe.

Three, four,
Knock at the door.

Five, six,
Pick up sticks.

Seven, eight,
Lay them straight.

Nine, ten,
A good, fat hen.

Eleven, twelve,
Dig and delve.

Thirteen, fourteen,
Maids a-courting.

Fifteen, sixteen,
Maids in the kitchen.

Seventeen, eighteen,
Maids a-waiting.

Nineteen, twenty,
My plate's empty.

HERE IS THE CHURCH

Here is the church,
Here is the steeple,
Open the doors,
And see all the people.

ELSIE MARLEY

Elsie Marley is grown so fine,
She won't get up,
To feed the swine.
But lies in bed,
'Til eight or nine,
Lazy Elsie Marley.

146

Frère Jacques

Frère Jacques.
Frère Jacques.

Dormez vous?
Dormez vous?

Sonnez les matines.
Sonnez les matines.

Ding, ding, dong.
Ding, ding, dong.

FEE, FIE, FOE, FUM!

Fee, Fie, Foe, Fum!
I smell the blood of an Englishman.
Be he alive or be he dead,
I'll grind his bones to make my bread.

EENIE, MEENIE, MINIE, MO

Eenie, meenie, minie, mo,
Catch a tiger by the toe.
If he hollers let him go,
Eenie, meenie, minie, mo.

Sippity, Sippity Sup

Sippity sup, sippity sup,
Bread and milk from a china cup.
Bread and milk from a bright silver spoon,
Made of a piece of the bright silver moon.
Sippity sup, sippity sup,
Sippity, sippity sup.

Bow, Wow, Wow

Bow, wow, wow,
Whose dog art thou?
Little Tom Tinker's dog,
Bow, wow, wow.

HICKORY DICKORY DOCK

Hickory dickory dock,
The mouse ran up the clock.
The clock struck one,
The mouse ran down,
Hickory dickory dock.

ONCE I SAW A LITTLE BIRD

Once l saw a little bird,
Go hop, hop, hop.
So I cried, little bird,
Will you stop, stop, stop?
And I was going to the window,
To say, how do you do?
When he shook his little tail,
And away he flew.

HORSIE, HORSIE

Horsie, horsie, don't you stop,
Just let your feet go clippety clop.
Your tail goes swish,
And the wheels go round,
Giddyup, you're homeward bound!

FOR WANT OF A NAIL

For want of a nail the shoe was lost.
For want of a shoe the horse was lost.
For want of a horse the rider was lost.
For want of a rider the battle was lost.
For want of a battle the kingdom was lost.
And all for the want of a horse shoe nail.

COBBLER, COBBLER

Cobbler, cobbler, mend my shoe.
Get it done by half-past two.
Stitch it up and stitch it down,
And then I'll give you half a crown.

153

A Needle And Thread

Old Mother Twitchett had but one eye,
And a long tail which she let fly,
And every time she went through a gap,
A bit of her tail she left in a trap.

THERE WAS AN OLD WOMAN

There was an old woman,
Who lived in a shoe.
She had so many children,
She didn't know what to do.
She gave them some broth,
Without any bread.
She whipped them all soundly,
And sent them to bed.

THE CATS WENT OUT

The cats went out to serenade,
And on a banjo sweetly played,
And summer nights they climbed a tree,
And sang, "My love, oh, come to me!"

LITTLE ROBIN REDBREAST

Little Robin Redbreast sat upon a tree,
Up went pussy cat, and down went he!
Down came pussy, and away Robin ran,
Says little Robin Redbreast, "Catch me if you can!"

THIS OLD MAN

This old man, he played one,
He played knick knack on my thumb.
With a knick knack paddy whack,
Give a dog a bone.
This old man came rolling home.

157

I Wriggle My Fingers

I wriggle my fingers,
I wriggle my toes.
I wriggle my shoulders,
I wriggle my nose.
No more wriggles are left in me,
So I will be as still as can be.

Do Your Ears Hang Low?

Do your ears hang low?
Do they wobble to and fro?
Can you tie 'em in a knot?
Can you tie 'em in a bow?
Can you throw them
Over your shoulder,
Like a continental soldier?
Do your ears hang low?

Do your ears flip flop?
Can you use them as a mop?
Are they stringy at the bottom?
Are they curly at the top?
Can you put them in a shower,
With a giant daisy flower?
Do your ears flip flop?

Does your tongue hang out?
Can you shake it all about?
When you try to tuck it in,
Does it just hang out?
Can you roll it to the ground,
With a clunk and a pound?
Does your tongue hang out?

159

JACK A NORY

I'll tell you a story about Jack A Nory,
And now my story's told.
I'll tell you another,
About Jack and his brother,
And now my story's done.